I, ____,

am committed to doing the work in order to combat racism,

change the world, and become a good ancestor.

me and white supremacy

a guided journal

The Official Companion to the
New York Times Bestselling Book
Me and White Supremacy

LAYLA F. SAAD

Published by Sourcebooks
P.O. Box 4410, Naperville, Illinois 60567-4410
(630) 961-3900
sourcebooks.com

Printed and bound in the United States of America.
VP 10 9 8 7 6 5 4 3

contents

create the change the world needs by creating change within yourself.

Dear Journaler,

Welcome to this guided journal, which serves as the official companion to *Me and White Supremacy: Combat Racism, Change the World, and Become a Good Ancestor*.

As the author of *Me and White Supremacy*, one of my intentions was to make it a book that you not only *read*, but also a book that you *do*. I believe that awareness leads to action, and action leads to change. But without the conscious awareness of how white supremacy operates in your unconscious thoughts, beliefs, and behaviors, it is difficult to practice antiracism in a meaningful way.

One of the most powerful ways to create conscious awareness is the practice of journaling, which is why it is a key feature of *Me and White Supremacy* and why I have created this guided journal to accompany it.

This guided journal includes all of the original journaling prompts for the twenty-eight-day journey laid out in *Me and White Supremacy*, with lots of space for note-taking and freewriting, as well as plenty of additional notes pages in the back. It is perfect to use whether you are working through *Me and White Supremacy* by yourself, with a partner, or in a group. And it will serve as a transformational antiracism tool that you can come back to again and again.

Use this journal as a mirror to look deep within yourself and see the truth of the ways in which you, often unconsciously, cause harm to Black, Indigenous, People of Color. Don't be afraid if what comes up sounds ugly or disgusting. Get it on the page so you can confront it, and change it.

This journal is for your eyes only. And by using it to dig deep and do the work, you are creating ripples of healing for us all. To be a good ancestor means to do the work that we must do in our lifetime so those who come after we are gone may benefit.

May the work you do in this journal create a multigenerational legacy of healing and liberation from white supremacy.

Thank you for a being a good ancestor.

WHO IS THIS WORK FOR?

Any person who holds white privilege. This includes persons who are biracial, multiracial, or white-passing People of Color who benefit under systems of white supremacy from having lighter skin color than visibly Brown, Black, or Indigenous people.

What You Will Need to Do This Work

- *Your truth*
- *Your love*
- *Your commitment*

HOW TO USE THIS JOURNAL

- **Read the chapter for the day in *Me and White Supremacy* first,** *then go through the journal questions after.*
- **Go at your own pace:** *While it has been designed as a twenty-eight-day challenge, you can go through* Me and White Supremacy *at your own pace, as fast or as slow as you choose.*
- **Don't generalize:** *When answering the prompts, do not generalize about white people broadly. This is about your own personal experiences, thoughts, and beliefs, not those of other people.*
- **I suggest working through the book sequentially,** *as each prompt builds upon the preceding one.*
- **After you've completed the work sequentially, work intuitively:** *You can either begin from Day 1, or you can dip in and out depending on what particular aspect of white supremacy is coming up for you to explore at that time.*
- **Work alone or with a group:** *See the Resources section at the end of* Me and White Supremacy *for more specific guidance on how to do this work in a group setting.*
- **Keep asking questions:** *Dig deeper by asking yourself when, how, and why questions that help you to get down into the deeper unconscious layers of your internalized white supremacy.*

here's to doing what is right and not what is easy.

WEEK 1 ◆ DAY 1

YOU AND WHITE PRIVILEGE

What is white privilege?

White privilege describes the unearned advantages that are granted because of one's whiteness or ability to "pass" as white.

DATE: / /

In what ways do you hold white privilege? Study the list from Peggy McIntosh on page 37 of the book and reflect on your own daily life. Make a list of the different ways you hold white privilege in your personal life.

DATE: / /

What negative experiences has your white privilege protected you from throughout your life?

DATE: / /

What positive experiences has your white privilege granted you throughout your life (that BIPOC generally do not have)?

DATE: / /

In what ways have you wielded your white privilege over BIPOC that have done harm (whether or not you intended to do so)?

DATE: / /

What have you learned about your white privilege that makes you uncomfortable?

WEEK 1 ◆ DAY 2

YOU AND WHITE FRAGILITY

What is white fragility?

Author Robin DiAngelo defines white fragility as "a state in which even a minimum amount of racial stress becomes intolerable, triggering a range of defensive moves."

DATE: / /

How does your white fragility show up during conversations about race? Do you fight, freeze, or flee?

DATE: / /

Describe your most visceral memory of experiencing white fragility. How old were you? Where were you? What was the conversation about? Why did it bring up white fragility in you? How do you recall feeling during and after the interaction? How do you feel about it today?

DATE: / /

How have you weaponized your fragility against BIPOC through, for example, calling the authorities, crying, or claiming you're being harmed ("Reverse racism!" or "I'm being shamed!" or "I'm being attacked!")?

DATE: / /

How do you feel when you hear the words *white people*? Do they make you feel uncomfortable?

DATE: / /

How has your white fragility prevented you, through fear and discomfort, from doing meaningful work around your own personal antiracism to date?

WEEK 1 ◆ DAY 3

YOU AND TONE POLICING

What is tone policing?

Tone policing is a tactic used by those who have privilege to silence those who do not by focusing on the tone of what is being said rather than the actual content.

DATE: / /

How have you used tone policing out loud to silence, shut down, or dismiss BIPOC? What kinds of words have you used to describe what tone a BIPOC should use?

DATE: / /

What tone policing thoughts have you harbored inside when you've heard BIPOC talk about race or their lived experiences, even if you didn't say them out loud?

DATE: / /

How have you derailed conversations about race by focusing on how someone said something to you rather than what they said to you? Looking back now, why do you think the tone that was being used was more important to you than the content of the information being conveyed?

DATE: / /

How often have you made your willingness to engage in antiracism work conditional on people using the "right" tone with you?

DATE: / /

How have you discounted BIPOC's real pain over racism because the way they talk about it doesn't fit with your worldview of how people should talk?

DATE: / /

How have you discounted BIPOC in general because of the tone they use when they talk?

tone policing reinforces white supremacist norms of how BIPOC are "supposed" to show up. it is a way of keeping BIPOC in line and disempowered.

WEEK 1 · DAY 4

YOU AND WHITE SILENCE

What is white silence?

White silence is when people with white privilege stay complicitly silent when it comes to issues of race and white supremacy.

DATE: / /

How have you stayed silent when it comes to race and racism?

DATE: / /

What types of situations elicit the most white silence from you?

DATE: / /

How has your silence been complicit in upholding racist behavior?

DATE: / /

How do you benefit from white silence?

DATE: / /

Whom in your life do you harm with your white silence?

WEEK 1 ✦ DAY 5

YOU AND WHITE SUPERIORITY

What is white superiority?

White superiority stems directly from white supremacy's belief that people with white or white-passing skin are better than and therefore deserve to dominate over people with brown or black skin.

DATE: / /

Think back across your life, from childhood to where you are in your life now. In what ways have you consciously or subconsciously believed that you are better than BIPOC?

Don't hide from this. This is the crux of white supremacy. Own it.

DATE: / /

DATE: / /

WEEK 1 ❖ DAY 6

YOU AND WHITE EXCEPTIONALISM

What is white exceptionalism?

White exceptionalism is the belief that you, as a person holding white privilege, are exempt from the effects, benefits, and conditioning of white supremacy and therefore that the work of antiracism does not really apply to you.

DATE: / /

In what ways have you believed that you are exceptional, exempt, “one of the good ones,” or above the conditioning of white supremacy?

DATE: / /

In what ways have you acted out of a sense of white exceptionalism when in racial conversations with BIPOC? (For example, when called out for unintentional racist behavior, have you tried to explain or demonstrate that you are "one of the good ones"?)

DATE: / /

Reread the extract from Martin Luther King Jr.'s letter and think back on the topics we have covered so far in *Me and White Supremacy*. How has your white exceptionalism prevented you from showing up in allyship to BIPOC?

First, I must confess that over the past few years I have been gravely disappointed with the white moderate. I have almost reached the regrettable conclusion that the Negro's great stumbling block in his stride toward freedom is not the White Citizen's Council-er or the Ku Klux Klanner, but the white moderate, who is more devoted to "order" than to justice; who prefers a negative peace which is the absence of tension to a positive peace which is the presence of justice; who constantly says: "I agree with you in the goal you seek, but I cannot agree with your methods of direct action"; who paternalistically believes he can set the timetable for another man's freedom; who lives by a mythical concept of time and who constantly advises the Negro to wait for a "more convenient season." Shallow understanding from people of good will is more frustrating than absolute misunderstanding from people of ill will. Lukewarm acceptance is much more bewildering than outright rejection.

DATE: / /

DATE: / /

Think back to your childhood. How did society (parents, schools, the media) teach you white exceptionalism?

DATE: / /

If you are a parent, in what ways are you teaching your children white exceptionalism?

the moment you begin to think you are exceptional is the moment you begin to relax back into the warm and familiar comfort of white supremacy.

WEEK 1 · DAY 7

REVIEW

On this reflection day, I want to remind you that we are not looking for the happy ending, the teachable moment, or the pretty bow at the end of all the learning. The aim of this work is truth—seeing it, owning it, and figuring out what to do with it. This is lifelong work.

DATE: / /

What have you begun to see and understand about your personal complicity in white supremacy that you were not able to see or understand before you began this work?

DATE: / /

DATE: / /

the aim of this work is truth—seeing it, owning it, and figuring out what to do with it. this is lifelong work.

this work is not just about changing how things look but how things actually are—from the inside out, one person, one family, one business, and one community at a time.

WEEK 2 ◆ DAY 8

YOU AND COLOR BLINDNESS

What is color blindness?

Race-based color blindness is the idea that you do not "see" color. That you do not notice differences in race. Or if you do, that you do not treat people differently or oppress people based on those differences.

DATE: / /

What messages were you taught about color blindness and seeing color growing up?

DATE: / /

How do you feel when BIPOC talk about race and racism?

DATE: / /

How have you harmed BIPOC in your life by insisting you do not see color?

DATE: / /

What is the first instinctual feeling that comes up when you hear the words *white people* or when you have to say *Black people*?

DATE: / /

What mental gymnastics have you done to avoid seeing your own race (and what those of white privilege have collectively done to BIPOC)?

For Days 9–11, we will be looking at anti-Blackness. Reread the note on anti-Blackness on page 84 of *Me and White Supremacy*.

WEEK 2 ◆ DAY 9

YOU AND ANTI-BLACKNESS AGAINST BLACK WOMEN

What is anti-Blackness against Black women?

Black women are often painted with a broad, monolithic brushstroke that categorizes them into particular stereotypes that rob them of their humanity, unique individuality, and worthiness.

DATE: / /

Think about the country you live in. What are some of the national racial stereotypes—spoken and unspoken, historic and modern—associated with Black women?

DATE: / /

What kinds of relationships have you had and do you have with Black women, and how deep are these relationships?

DATE: / /

How do you think about Black women who are citizens in your country differently from those who are recent immigrants?

DATE: / /

How have you treated darker-skinned Black women differently from lighter-skinned Black women?

DATE: / /

What are some of the stereotypes you have thought and negative assumptions you have made about Black women, and how have these affected how you have treated them?

DATE: / /

How have you expected Black women to serve or soothe you?

DATE: / /

How have you reacted in the presence of Black women who are unapologetic in their confidence, self-expression, boundaries, and refusal to submit to the white gaze?

DATE: / /

How have you excluded, discounted, minimized, used, tone policed, or projected your white fragility and white superiority onto Black women?

you cannot change your white skin color to stop receiving these privileges, just like BIPOC cannot change their skin color to stop receiving racism. but what you *can* do is wake up to what is really going on.

WEEK 2 • DAY 10

YOU AND ANTI-BLACKNESS AGAINST BLACK MEN

What is anti-Blackness against Black men?

Black men are often trapped in a one-dimensional imagining of what and who they are supposed to be, stripping them of their humanity.

DATE: / /

Think about the country you live in. What are some of the national racial stereotypes—spoken and unspoken, historic and modern—associated with Black men?

DATE: / /

How do you think about Black men who are citizens in your country differently from those who are recent immigrants?

DATE: / /

What kinds of relationships have you had and do you have with Black men, and how deep are these relationships?

DATE: / /

How have you treated darker-skinned Black men differently from lighter-skinned Black men?

DATE: / /

What are some of the stereotypes you have thought and negative assumptions you have made about Black men, and how have they affected how you have treated them?

DATE: / /

How have you excluded, discounted, minimized, used, tone policed, or projected your white fragility and white superiority onto Black men?

DATE: / /

How have you fetishized Black men?

DATE: / /

How much freedom do you give Black men in your mind to be complex and multilayered human beings?

tell the truth, as deeply as you can.

WEEK 2 ◆ DAY 11

YOU AND ANTI-BLACKNESS AGAINST BLACK CHILDREN

What is anti-Blackness against Black children?

Black children in the white imagination often start out as cute. And then at some point, they grow up, and in the white imagination, they are suddenly not so cute anymore. Anti-Blackness and the adultification of Black children results in Black children not being treated as children but rather as the adult Black people they will grow up to be in the white imagination.

DATE: / /

Think about the country you live in. What are some of the national racial stereotypes—spoken and unspoken, historic and modern—associated with Black children?

DATE: / /

How do you think about Black children who are citizens in your country differently from those who are recent immigrants?

DATE: / /

How have you viewed or do you view Black children when they are young versus when they get to their teens and young adulthood?

DATE: / /

How have you treated Black children differently from white children? And how have you treated darker-skinned Black children differently from lighter-skinned Black children?

DATE: / /

How have you tokenized and fetishized “cute Black kids” or “cute mixed kids”?

DATE: / /

How have you wanted to "save" Black children?

DATE: / /

If you are a white or biracial parent of Black children, what antiracism work have you been doing on yourself and in your communities to make the world a safe space for your children? Do you protect your kids when someone others your Black children, or do you retreat into white silence?

WEEK 2 ◆ DAY 12

YOU AND RACIST STEREOTYPES

What are racist stereotypes?

Racist stereotypes serve to maintain nonwhite people as the "other," the ones who should be feared, ridiculed, marginalized, criminalized, and dehumanized.

DATE: / /

What have you learned about you and racist stereotypes? Begin by making a list of the different racial groups of people found in your country. Where possible, break these down into countries.

DATE: / /

What are some of the national racial stereotypes in your country—spoken and unspoken, historic and modern—associated with Indigenous people and non-Black POC?

DATE: / /

What are the racist stereotypes, beliefs, and thoughts you hold about the different racial groups of people? In what ways do you paint them all with one brush rather than seeing them as complex individuals?

DATE: / /

How do you think about POC who are citizens in your country differently from those who are recent immigrants? How do you think about those who are more assimilated versus those who are less assimilated (e.g., if they practice your country's social norms, if they have accents that sound like yours, etc.)?

DATE: / /

How do you think about and treat Indigenous children and non-Black children of color differently from white children?

DATE: / /

How do you think about and treat darker-skinned Indigenous people and POC differently from those who are lighter-skinned?

DATE: / /

In what ways have you superhumanized parts of the identities of Indigenous people and POC while dehumanizing other parts?

WEEK 2 DAY 13

YOU AND CULTURAL APPROPRIATION

What is cultural appropriation?

Cultural appropriation can include the appropriation of another culture's objects, motifs, symbols, rituals, artifacts, and other cultural elements that occurs between a dominant and a nondominant or marginalized culture.

DATE: / /

How have you or do you appropriate from nonwhite cultures?

DATE: / /

What actions have you taken when you have seen other white people culturally appropriating? Have you called it out? Or have you used your white silence?

DATE: / /

Have you been called out for cultural appropriation? How did you respond?

DATE: / /

How have you profited (socially or financially) from cultural appropriation?

DATE: / /

How have you excused cultural appropriation as being "not that bad"? How do you feel about it now having done thirteen days of this work?

WEEK 2 ◆ DAY 14

REVIEW

This week of the work was heavy. Ugly. You learned that white supremacy is a set of subtle behaviors, thoughts, and beliefs, often unconscious, that when put together make up a really scary jigsaw puzzle. It is not enough to look at just one or two pieces of the jigsaw. To see the whole picture, we have to look at each piece in turn and see the entire story being told.

DATE: / /

What have you begun to see that you can't unsee?

DATE: / /

What have you begun to unearth about yourself when it comes to white supremacy?

DATE: / /

What have these last thirteen days (and especially the last six days) shown you about how white supremacy works through you?

DATE: / /

What have you learned about the dehumanizing ways you think about and treat BIPOC and why?

DATE: / /

What have you learned about you and anti-Blackness?

DATE: / /

If you are biracial, multiracial, or a Person of Color holding white privilege, what has this week brought up for you? How can you find grounding and self-care for yourself after this heavy week?

DATE: / /

If you came to this book thinking you were "one of the good white people" or an ally to BIPOC, how do you feel about that now?

DATE: / /

How are you thinking differently about your white privilege, white fragility, white tone policing, white silence, white superiority, and white exceptionalism now?

challenging emotions like shame, anger, grief, rage, apathy, anxiety, and confusion will come up for you if you are doing this work deeply. don't run away from those feelings. feeling the feelings is an important part of the process.

WEEK 3 ◆ DAY 15

YOU AND WHITE APATHY

What is white apathy?

White apathy is the detachment and indifference to racial harm that arises as a self-preservation response to protect yourself from having to face your complicity in the oppression that is white supremacy.

DATE: / /

In what ways have you been apathetic when it comes to racism?

DATE: / /

In what ways have you observed people who hold white privilege in your communities (family, friends, work) being apathetic when it comes to racism?

white apathy lacks aggression, but it is deadly in its passivity.

WEEK 3 ◆ DAY 16

YOU AND WHITE CENTERING

What is white centering?

White centering is the centering of white people, white values, white norms, and white feelings over everything and everyone else.

DATE: / /

How is your worldview a white-centered one?

DATE: / /

How have you reacted when whiteness or you as a white person are not centered in spaces and conversations?

DATE: / /

How have you judged BIPOC when they do not measure up to white-centered standards?

DATE: / /

How have you centered yourself as a person with white privilege in non-white spaces and conversations?

DATE: / /

What are you beginning to understand about how white centering affects BIPOC?

WEEK 3 ◆ DAY 17

YOU AND TOKENISM

What is tokenism?

Tokenism essentially uses BIPOC as props or meaningless symbols to make it look like antiracism is being practiced while continuing to maintain the status quo of white as the dominant norm.

DATE: / /

How have you justified your racism by using your proximity to BIPOC?

DATE: / /

How have you tokenized BIPOC to prove your words, thoughts, or actions are not racist?

DATE: / /

How have you tokenized and weaponized one BIPOC against another BIPOC?

DATE: / /

If you are a business owner, how have you tokenized BIPOC or BIPOC culture in your brand?

DATE: / /

If you believe you have never tokenized BIPOC, how have you stayed silent when you saw it happening?

DATE: / /

When you have lauded organizations or events for being diverse because they appear to have a few BIPOC, how much further have you looked into their actual practices and policies toward BIPOC? How have you mistaken the look of diversity for actual inclusivity and equity?

tokenism looks flattering on the outside, but the truth of it is that it uses BIPOC as if they are things, not people.

WEEK 3 ◆ DAY 18

YOU AND WHITE SAVIORISM

What is white saviorism?

The belief that people with white privilege, who see themselves as superior in capability and intelligence, have an obligation to "save" BIPOC from their supposed inferiority and helplessness.

DATE: / /

What white savior narratives have you noticed yourself buying into (whether consciously or unconsciously)?

DATE: / /

In what ways have you believed that BIPOC are helpless and require intervention and help from people with white privilege?

DATE: / /

In what ways have you tried to intervene or offer instruction or guidance, believing that your (superior white) view would offer the best solutions?

DATE: / /

In what ways have you spoken over BIPOC or for them because you felt that you could explain their needs and experiences better than they could? In what ways have you put BIPOC words through a white filter?

DATE: / /

How have you unconsciously thought about dismantling racism as something that you needed to give your "help" to as a good white savior?

DATE: / /

What has your reaction been when BIPOC have told you or other people with white privilege that they do not need your "help" and that instead they need you to listen, do the work, and follow BIPOC leadership? What reactions have you noticed coming up (e.g., white fragility, tone policing, white exceptionalism, white superiority, etc.)?

the purpose of this
work is not for you to
end up living in shame.
the purpose is to get
you to see the truth
so that you can do
something about it.

WEEK 3 ◇ DAY 19

YOU AND OPTICAL ALLYSHIP

What is optical allyship?

Latham Thomas, author and founder of Mama Glow, defines *optical allyship* as "allyship that only serves at the surface level to platform the 'ally,' it makes a statement but doesn't go beneath the surface and is not aimed at breaking away from the systems of power that oppress."

DATE: / /

How have you practiced optical allyship when it comes to antiracism?

DATE: / /

What benefits have you sought out and/or received by practicing optical allyship?

DATE: / /

How have you responded when called out for optical allyship?

DATE: / /

How have you felt when you have not been rewarded for your acts of optical allyship?

DATE: / /

How has your motivation to show up in allyship been dependent upon what other people think about you or how you are perceived?

WEEK 3 ◆ DAY 20

YOU AND BEING CALLED OUT/CALLED IN

What is being called out or called in?

Call outs and calls in are both methods of calling attention to problematic, harmful, and oppressive behaviors with the ultimate aim being changed behavior and the making of amends.

DATE: / /

What have you felt, thought, said, or done when called out/in? How have you centered yourself and your intentions over BIPOC and the impact of your actions?

DATE: / /

If it has not happened to you yet, how do you think you will react when it happens, based on your level of self-awareness, personal antiracism work, and white fragility?

DATE: / /

When you have been called out/in, how have you handled apologizing and making amends?

DATE: / /

What are your biggest fears about being called out/in?

DATE: / /

Think back over the topics we have covered so far in this book. What behaviors and beliefs most get in your way of being able to respond appropriately to being called out/in?

WEEK 3 ◆ DAY 21

REVIEW

This week, we covered behaviors related to the practice of allyship and how white supremacy can continue to be perpetuated in actions and behaviors that seem noble or neutral in theory but quickly reveal a foundation of the racist status quo being maintained underneath. Maya Angelou famously said, "Do the best you can until you know better. Then when you know better, do better."

DATE: / /

What more have you learned about yourself and your unique, personal brand of white supremacy?

DATE: / /

In what ways have you realized behaviors you have thought were "not that bad" were actually very harmful?

DATE: / /

Where are you beginning to see your biggest challenge is when it comes to your personal antiracism work?

DATE: / /

Where are you starting to do your work, and where are you still holding back?

DATE: / /

What other dots have you started connecting when reflecting on the work you have done so far?

WEEK 4 ◆ DAY 22

YOU AND WHITE FEMINISM

What is white feminism?

White feminism focuses on the struggles of white women (usually cisgendered) over BIPOC. It is a feminism that is only concerned with disparities and oppression of gender, and it does not take into account disparities and oppression of other intersections, including race, class, age, ability, sexual orientation, gender identity, and so on.

DATE: / /

To what extent has your idea of feminism been under the issue of gender only?

DATE: / /

How has your feminism neglected or minimized the issues of BIPOC?

DATE: / /

How has your feminism rejected, discounted, or simply ignored BIPOC leaders?

DATE: / /

How has your feminism been white-centered?

DATE: / /

If you are someone who has called yourself an intersectional feminist, in what ways have you been centering BIWOC?

WEEK 4 • DAY 23

YOU AND WHITE LEADERS

Today, we are looking at you and white leaders, specifically people with white privilege in positions of leadership, authority, and power with whom you come into contact.

DATE: / /

Knowing what you now know about white supremacist behaviors across Days 1–22, how do you respond when you witness white leaders behaving in these white supremacist ways:

- *When white leaders tone police BIPOC?*
- *When white leaders claim color blindness?*
- *When white leaders use anti-Black tropes or racist stereotypes?*
- *When white leaders practice cultural appropriation?*
- *When white leaders practice optical allyship and white saviorism?*

DATE: / /

DATE: / /

DATE: / /

When you have witnessed white leaders practicing these behaviors, how do your own white fragility and white silence get in the way of you asking them to do better?

there is no clean,
comfortable,
or convenient way
to dismantle
a violent system
of oppression.

**you must roll
up your sleeves and
get down into the
ugly, fertile dirt.**

DATE: / /

How does your fear of loss of privilege and comfort hold you back from asking white leaders to do better?

DATE: / /

How aware have you been of whether white leaders you follow are doing deeper antiracism work? How much of a priority has it been for you to push them to go beyond the visual effect of diversity?

DATE: / /

If you are in a leadership position, how do you plan to respond to your own behaviors going forward? How do you plan to hold yourself accountable to doing better?

WEEK 4 ◆ DAY 24

YOU AND YOUR FRIENDS

Today, we are continuing to look at the personal connections you have and how you respond when you notice white supremacist behaviors playing out with your friends.

DATE: / /

How have you responded when you have witnessed racist words and actions from these people in your life?

DATE: / /

How have you stayed silent or made excuses for them in your mind?

DATE: / /

How have you thought it was not worth the hassle because of the discomfort of rocking the boat? Or how have you seen it as your responsibility to address it with them since you have more influence over them because of your friendship?

DATE: / /

Are there certain people you feel more comfortable speaking up to than others? Why is that?

DATE: / /

Are there certain people you continue to stay in friendships with even though they are problematic and refuse to change?

DATE: / /

How have you risked these relationships by calling in/out racist behavior, even if nobody was going to thank you for it?

DATE: / /

How do you feel about your friends who are not doing their own personal antiracism work?

DATE: / /

What efforts have you made to invite your friends into doing antiracism work with you?

DATE: / /

How have you allowed your friends to influence you *not* to engage in anti-racism work?

WEEK 4 • DAY 25

YOU AND YOUR FAMILY

Your family is where you hold a great deal of influence. And with your more nuanced understanding of how liberal people with white privilege are also complicit in white supremacy from doing this work, you are in a powerful position to help your family members expand and deepen their own antiracism knowledge and practice too.

DATE: / /

How do you feel about speaking up about racism and white supremacist beliefs and actions to your family members?

DATE: / /

How have you excused or ignored your family members' racist behaviors because addressing them seems too difficult and you want to keep the peace?

DATE: / /

How have you excused your elders' racism because they are "from another time"?

DATE: / /

If you are a parent, how do you speak to your children about racism beyond "we don't see color"? How early did you or will you speak to your children about racism and white privilege? How early did your parents or caregivers speak to you about racism and white privilege?

DATE: / /

What racist beliefs have you internalized from your family?

DATE: / /

To what extent do you place white comfort over antiracism in your family?

DATE: / /

What are some ways in which you can begin to have deeper conversations with your family about racism?

DATE: / /

How do you allow perfectionism to get in the way of having racial conversations with your family?

DATE: / /

In what ways do you (or can you) organize your family to show up for BIPOC in your communities? Not from a place of white saviorism but rather by volunteering at and donating to antiracist movements and organizations being led by BIPOC in your communities?

WEEK 4 ◆ DAY 26

YOU AND YOUR VALUES

As you look at your values, I invite you to release the desire to be *seen* as good by other people and instead explore what it looks like for you to own that you are a person who holds privilege and that you are a person who is committed to practicing antiracism.

DATE: / /

To what extent have your values helped your ability to practice antiracism?

DATE: / /

What contradictory values do you hold that hinder your ability to practice antiracism?

DATE: / /

What new core values and beliefs do you feel you need to integrate after doing this work in order to better practice lifelong antiracism?

DATE: / /

How has your desire to be seen as a good person with white privilege prevented you from actually being "good"?

you will make mistakes. use these moments as opportunities to listen, apologize, become more educated about privilege and oppression, and do better going forward.

WEEK 4 ◆ DAY 27

YOU AND LOSING PRIVILEGE

In order for change to happen, you must lose some of your white privilege. I am talking about the privileges, advantages, and comforts you must be willing to let go of so that BIPOC can have more dignity in their lives.

DATE: / /

In what ways will your privilege need to change in order for you to consistently practice antiracism?

DATE: / /

How will you need to change the way you take up space for and with BIPOC?

DATE: / /

How will you need to show up differently for BIPOC?

DATE: / /

What risks must you be willing to take? What sacrifices must you be willing to make?

DATE: / /

What comforts must you be willing to lose?

DATE: / /

In what ways will you need to take greater responsibility?

DATE: / /

How will you need to decenter whiteness and the white gaze?

DATE: / /

How will you need to lose privilege and safety in your friendships, work-spaces, businesses, families, spiritual communities, and other white-centered spaces?

DATE: / /

Are you willing to lose your white privilege after everything you've learned here?

WEEK 4 ◆ DAY 28

YOU AND YOUR COMMITMENTS

Today, we are looking at what commitments you are ready to make to practice lifelong antiracism.

DATE: / /

Write three concrete, out-of-your-comfort-zone actions you are committed to taking in the next two weeks toward antiracism.

These could be uncomfortable conversations you need to have, significant changes in your life you need to make, someone you need to call out/in, sincere apologies you need to make, announcements you need to make, organizations you need to begin volunteering at, etc. Make these actions as *specific* as possible (what, where, when, how, who, why, etc.) and also make clear how you will be held accountable for these actions (e.g., choose and notify an accountability partner).

DATE: / /

DATE: / /

DATE: / /

DATE: / /

Starting today and over the next week, begin to write down your commitments to this work. Craft a commitments statement that you will be able to refer to every day and especially on the days when you forget, make mistakes, or begin to slip back into white apathy. Your commitments are not what you will try to do or hope to do but what you will do.

To craft this document, go back through all the days of this work and recall the ways you have done harm and the ways in which you are committed to change. Think about what you are ready to commit to in your personal life, your family life, your friendships, your work and business life, and your community life.

Use any or all of the following writing prompts to help you craft your commitment statement:

- *I am committed to showing up for this lifelong antiracism work because...*
- *I am committed to challenging my white fragility by...*
- *I am committed to using my voice for antiracism work by...*
- *I am committed to challenging racism in other people with white privilege by...*
- *I am committed to uplifting, supporting, and centering BIPOC by...*
- *I am committed to financially supporting the following BIPOC movements and causes...*
- *I am committed to decentering myself as a person with white privilege by...*
- *I am committed to continuing my lifelong antiracism education by...*

DATE: / /

- *I am committed to the following values that will help me to practice antiracism…*
- *I am committed to breaking through my white apathy by…*
- *I am committed to showing up even when I make mistakes by…*
- *I am committed to using my privilege for antiracism by…*
- *I am committed to challenging my optical allyship by…*
- *I am committed to being a good ancestor by…*

DATE: / /

DATE: / /

DATE: / /

DATE: / /

Remember: You do not have to write it all down today. Begin today but continue this over the coming days, weeks, months, and years. Your commitment statement is not a solid document set in stone. Treat it as a living, breathing, evolving, and ever-deepening statement that reflects your own growth in this work and your commitment to antiracism as a lifelong practice.

i invite you not
to run away from
the pain but to
allow it to break
your heart open.

closing note from layla

After twenty-eight days of reflective journaling and inner excavation, you now have a strong foundation to continue moving forward in your practice of antiracism. Your writing has revealed to you what you needed to see about your personal complicity and relationship with white supremacy.

Recognize that this journal gave you a first layer of revelations. There are many more layers to go. To get to these deeper layers and to unpack even further, buy yourself a new journal, and when you are ready, begin the twenty-eight days again. Use this journal as a resource for you to take responsibility for doing your own work.

As we close up our time together, I want to speak to the good ancestor who lies within you, the person inside you who came to do this work with questions about dismantling white supremacy and who leaves this work knowing that you are a part of the problem and that you are simultaneously also a part of the answer. There is great power and responsibility in that knowledge. But knowledge without action is meaningless.

No matter who you are, you have the power to influence change in the world. You can continue to unconsciously allow white supremacy to use you as it used your ancestors. Or you can intentionally choose to disrupt and dismantle white supremacy within yourself and your communities so that BIPOC can live free of racism and oppression.

The choice is yours. The moment is now.

Help change the world. Become a good ancestor.

notes

DATE: / /

DATE: / /

DATE: / /

DATE: / /

DATE: / /

DATE: / /

DATE: / /

DATE: / /

DATE: / /

DATE: / /

DATE: / /

DATE: / /

DATE: / /

DATE: / /

DATE: / /

DATE: / /

DATE: / /

DATE: / /

DATE: / /

DATE: / /

DATE: / /

DATE: / /

DATE: / /

DATE: / /

DATE: / /

DATE: / /

DATE: / /

DATE: / /

DATE: / /

DATE: / /

DATE: / /

DATE: / /

DATE: / /

DATE: / /

DATE: / /

DATE: / /

DATE: / /

DATE: / /

DATE: / /

DATE: / /

DATE: / /

DATE: / /

DATE: / /

DATE: / /

DATE: / /

DATE: / /

DATE: / /

DATE: / /

DATE: / /

DATE: / /

DATE: / /

DATE: / /

DATE: / /

DATE: / /

DATE: / /

DATE: / /

DATE: / /

DATE: / /

DATE: / /

DATE: / /

DATE: / /

DATE: / /

DATE: / /

DATE: / /

DATE: / /

DATE: / /

DATE: / /

DATE: / /

DATE: / /

DATE: / /

DATE: / /

DATE: / /

DATE: / /

DATE: / /

DATE: / /

DATE: / /

DATE: / /